ESSAY ON WATER

a book of poems

by

Victor Pearn

Indian Paintbrush Poets *Fort Collins Colorado*

poems in this collection have been published previously, sometimes in other versions in the following journals: *The Caribbean Writer, Abandoned Mine, Short Edition Water at Michigan State University, The Coloradan, The Scrivener, The Seventh Quarry, Evening Street Press, Cider Press Review, The Midwest Quarterly, Pembroke Magazine, Plowman Press Canada, Kindred Spirit Press, Tiny Moments and Haight Ashbury Literary Journal.* "living inside confucius wall" appeared originally translated to Mandarin and published by Jining University Qufu, China, 2009.

Essay on Water

Copyright © 2025 by Victor Pearn

First Edition

All rights reserved

ISBN   978-1-7357731-4-8

Published by
Indian Paintbrush Poets, 3518 Kingston Cir
Fort Collins, Colorado 80525

Manufactured in the United States of America

Cover design by Megan Ryan

*for Crystal, Cynthia, Spirit, February,
Ragen, Ashlyn, Kayley and Grace*

I sit on a man's back choking him and making him carry me, and yet assure myself and others that I am very very sorry for him and wish to lighten his load — except by getting off his back.

Leo Tolstoy

Contents

  Mr. Raven

SURF RETURNS

  As You Snooze 1
  Dawn At Oahu 2
  They Will Know Us By Our Love 3
  Anthropology 5
  Duffy 6
  Lapsis Lazuli 10
  Listening To The Surf 11
  Surfing After Work 13
  Surfing East Oahu 14
  Who's In Heaven 15
  With Flowers In Her Hair 16
  Splashing Water 18
  Girls Surfing 19
  Honolulu Days 20
  Shapley's Heavenly Bodies 22
  The Surfer Dude 23
  Essay On Water 24
  Surf Returns 28

MADRID, CHINA, AND OTHER PLACES

  Plaza Mayor Madrid 1974 39
  My College Roommate 42
  Fifteenth Child 45
  Living Inside Confucius Wall 46
  Tigers Of The Chinese Calendar 47

Pyromaniac   48
Encounters At The Washing Machine
    During A Pandemic   49
Integrity   50
The Café   51
Simpler Days   52
Original Description   53
The Umber Haze Of Summer   54
Epiphany   55
Erecting A New Memorial   56
Illinois & Times   57
Janet Hard   58
Joy   60
Leo   61
Emerald Rainbow   62
Pie   63
Spoon River   64
The 1966 24-Hour Le Mans Trophy   65
The Willow   67

WALKING IN SNOW BEFORE DAWN

Ducklings   71
Driving A Tractor At Seven   72
Columbine   74
And What Truth Makes Something Out Of
    Nothing   75
Baseball   76
Micro Screenplay   77
2020 Census   78
Cello & Guitar   79
Bunny   80

At First Light   81
Apache   82
Balanced Rock   83
On Deer Mountain   85
Pile Burning   86
Reporting My Pint To The IRS   87
Twin Sisters Mountain Peak   88
Walking In Snow Before Dawn   89
"Publishing books people love reading."

Mr Raven

is born with wings
five fingers no thumbs
while studying at
the university of alabama
his wife types
his thesis on the work of
william shakespeare

moss hangs on tree limbs
in florida at auburndale high where
mr raven begins teaching seniors
he tells us these stories of home life
one morning his son falls
against the corner of a coffee table
knocking two front teeth
completely out and unbelievably
he does it again
in the same place punching out
two more front teeth

in moonlight past calm lakes
actors from new york companies
perform here in community colleges
plays mr raven reads aloud in class
three immortal plays by shakespeare
explaining nuances in every word
how words change over time
in inference and meaning
and mr raven gives us free tickets
and helps me learn about creativity

SURF RETURNS

As You Snooze

in and out in and out
I listen to the rhythm
of your breathing
as your steady lungs fill
then exhale in an unchanging cycle
you hug me for warmth
and trying to make yourself
more comfortable
scrunch my body like a pillow
indefinitely beside you

Dawn At Oahu

Along the shore
a deep purple cloud
a glimpse of lovely sunlight
casting orange through purple clouds.

As it hit the edge of the Pacific
and became a fiery orange giant,
the indigo sea licked up surf
with bubbly white waves.

A few gulls stood along the shore.
The sun peeked out of a deep purple cloud,
As the earth turned toward it
sunlight became golden.

A pelican skimmed the surface.
Surf crested with golden light
as it flipped bubbled white foam leaving
a magic pink glow on wet white sand.

A row of coconut bearing palms
line the shore gently waving
their green Hawaiian fronds
in rhythm with the sound of the surf.

For They Will Know Us By Our Love
for Paul Levitt

"I preferred verse to fame, but I wrote with the heart of an amateur."
From *Omeros*, by Derek Walcott

Blood of Vietnam is on this boot. Measuring the speed of loss, Kuwait, Iraq, Afghanistan an historic war lineage, more blood on this boot. Building new prisons. Spending more on inmates than students. Bombs deafening bombs, annihilating until ending what cannot be measured. How to stop building bombs, how to stop manufacturing weapons, watering the earth with human blood.
Put down your automatic rifles. Stop making bullets. Replace anger with calm. What does the ocean sound like? The only planet known to have oceans. A tiny wet speck floating in the universe. Among enormous, fiercely burning, fiery stars, there's this gentle rhythm, waves washing up on shore, birds singing, the sunset glow golden and pink on the grey shaded and white billowing clouds. Fifty-two states form a more perfect union, Puerto Rico the fifty-first and Washington DC the fifty-second. Poetry is Satyagraha, is nonviolent resistance, and Satyagraha is poetry in circles of talk. Circles of talk is nonviolent resistance. A boy being raised by a single mother was alone until a neighbor girl his age became his friend. They swam, they walked, they went to the movies and ate vanilla ice cream in crystal dishes smothered with chocolate syrup. They lived in young love unfettered with grown up entanglements. She lived in another city near the Mississippi River visiting her grandparents two houses south for two or three

summers until her grandparents passed away and she did not return. The next summer the young man tried out for pony league baseball and made outfielder for the Hertzberg New Method book bindery team. Friends both grew up and went on their way. But that summer he played alone in the outfield, riding his bicycle to every game, playing his heart out, missing her. She was gone, but love remained strong. Everybody has a story to tell. An ocean voyage. Watching the moon descend below the surface of the ocean and the sky turn. A double rainbow arched high above the island and again, he flew home, to level prairies and gently flowing rivers in the Midwest. As autumn paints October leaves, "I've seen fire and I've seen rain." How then can you honor God? By being kind to the greedy, yes, by being kind, being kind to the needy. In this you honor God. For they will know us by our love; they will know us by our love; black while stars in cloud like clumps swirled dancing overhead. Water from the west illuminated dazzling bright blue as he sat alone on the beach and the soft wind swayed the palm fronds. The ocean from underneath the surface, grew brighter and gradually dimmed, until the reflecting moonlight was gone and the water was dark in the shadow of the night. That night he thought about where she might be as he walked barefooted in the moist sand. He carried Pam Ruby in his heart, then it was light. In dawn there was a great fragrance, sweet flowers in rain fresh air.

Anthropology

It cannot be a cheap black suit;
in stark reality to surfing
a wave so big no one will go in the
water. Because words are sharp teeth.

We The People,
from every region of this planet—
in every ethnic group, in every native
village there are unique traits
outside the norm of that group.

The only question that we can ask
should be—who did you know in your
neighborhood—or medically speaking,
what is your blood type? And well,
even that differs in surfing families

Duffy

Friday after duty
hitchhiking
in civilian clothes
carrying backpacks
in Kaneohe Bay,
miles from North Shore beach,
we took our time walking
along the busy streets.
Duffy had a guitar
and sometimes he'd softly
sing pop tunes
in the squad bay.
It was there that
we'd discussed going
on a camping trip
together for a weekend
to the legendary beach we'd
only heard about, not seen.
In our backpacks
we'd each brought a
marine half-tent shelter,
 to sleep on shore under stars.
We were holding
a nickel bag of pretty
weak weed. It looked
like it was cut with straw,
but delivered a buzz.
That evening we
got off the main highway
and were heading down
a red dirt road going through

fresh ripe pineapple fields.
As far as you could see
in any direction there were
only rows after rows of pineapple.
Not a single car or home,
no light anywhere—and
in darkness—the visible sky
was a magnificent star cluster.
Eventually pineapple fields stopped
and we discovered North Shore.
We put our tent up
well past midnight,
unrolled the blankets,
and were fast asleep.
That may have been
the darkest and loneliest
place on Earth that night.
We were surprised
by the morning light
as we woke to low grey clouds
and an empty beach.
Across the road a little
mom and pop grocery store
provided us with coffee,
donuts, and snack food.
Alone on the beach
after breakfast, waves
rose to as high as five feet.
Body surfing, you'd
walk out waist deep,
then swim to the wave
where it swelled, turn, and surf
all the way back to the shore.

There was a strong undertow
five feet before you would
hit the beach. It pulled you
in a big rip current out
all the way to where
the wave rose.
You could relax, float
backwards into the Pacific
and catch the next wave.
If you wanted to get out
of the water you'd swim
hard toward shore the last
seven or eight feet in.
We stopped surfing for lunch.
You could eat homemade bread,
sandwiches, get a soda
from an entrepreneurial hippie who
sold them from his truck-van.
He recommended tuna salad,
he made it without tuna,
out of soy, and those were the best
and the most delicious
sandwiches we'd ever eaten.
It was one of those solid grey days.
We packed up our tent
and headed further along Oahu
on the curving highway to a bar.
We ordered draft beer in mugs.
There was an older man
sitting in the bar, who would work
for six months picking pineapple
each year, here in red dirt fields,
then go back to Alaska

on a tuna boat, working six months.
It was his life.
Leaving the bar we caught a bus
back to civilization,
first into Honolulu, and then
going through the tunnel
under the mountains back home
to the Marine Air Base at Kaneohe.
Shortly afterwards my discharge
papers arrived and I left Oahu.

Lapis Lazuli

Lines of fresh cut hay or clover
filled the clear morning
with a deep and sweet aroma
across dreaming farm meadows.
A lapis lazuli sky surrounded
the western pregnant moon—

I abandoned my dress uniform in Kaneohe Bay.
At San Francisco with no surfboard,
studying waves roiling just south of
Golden Gate Bridge, I left meditating.
If only I'd brought a board from Oahu.
I'd flown off the island, out of the Marine
Crotch (as my Polynesian DI called it in boot
camp), and the choice waves were dark.

Listening to the Surf

> "I was so much older then.
> I'm younger than that now."
> —Bob Dylan

Woke in intensive care
beside a marine brigadier general,
we both had left nephrectomies.
As my eyes opened, my sister Sara
prayed beside me, and I was alive.
The nurse made me stand up.
Later that day the general told me
he wore his hair short because
it was cool in his fighter-pilot helmet.

We were in Tripler General
a pink army hospital on Oahu.
Growing my beard after surgery,
unheard of in the marines.
When an officer came to my room
he said I couldn't return to duty
unless I shaved my beard.
The head nurse, a male captain,
said I should stay at the army hospital.
I returned to the marine air base.

Stronger each morning,
feeling more healthy than
I'd ever felt in my life before,
I began rising with mental clarity
in the middle of the night,
writing descriptions of cumulus clouds,

colorful rainbows, then sharing
poems with fellow marines.

And there's nothing like:
surfing on this lovely emerald island,
walking with a surfboard
under swaying palm fronds
into the gentle breeze,
listening to the surf,
paddling out trying to catch a wave.

Surfing After Work

We were off duty at five p.m.
every day I would go out
on the sandy shores of Kaneohe Bay, Oahu
my Marine Air Base.
All I had to do, in my cubicle,
was quickly change
into brightly flowered swimming shorts,
put on my flip-flops, grab the board
and walk 300 yards to the beach.

Our surfboard was a 7'0" yellow
with a real marijuana leaf
the size of a large outspread hand
embedded under a clear surface
in the board's center.
We only had one board in our squad bay.
It belonged to another marine
that would allow anyone use it, but
I was the only other one who surfed;
he rolled weed into joints.

He would smoke a joint
while showering, and wash the evidence
down the drain, but our captain,
going in fully dressed, caught him.
As they struggled the draftee won,
and the roach washed down a drain.
There were 42 marines in our squad bay,
40 of us smoked weed.

Surfing East Oahu

Fighting the ocean
on a slender board
for a short ride,
sometimes all you can do
is go on your knees.
Water moving up behind
can become like a cliff
threatening to swallow you,
maul you, and possibly rip
you far from your board.
Jellyfish membranes the size of
quarters or half dollars,
float everywhere, plentiful
as ocean bubbles. Beneath
the surface, a breeding-ground
with ten-thousand hungry
young swimmers—sharks—not the
type that would attack, but their
presence is uncomfortably frightening.

Who's in Heaven?

> "One two three four five six seven,
> all good children go to heaven."
> —The Beatles

John and George are practicing
magnificent guitar music,
and John is playing piano.

And they're writing new lyrics.

In perfect timing, waiting
for that moment to arrive when

they'll be reunited
with Paul and Ringo,
forever in Elysium clouds.

Imagine the concerts we'll hear.

With Flowers In Her Hair

Longboard surfing on Waikiki,
where beginners learn to ride
easy flowing waves. Judy arrived
the day before from Illinois,
and we lodged at a royal pink
hotel near Diamond Head.

Wisdom shouted
on the streets of Honolulu,
dressed in a white robe
she cried out to passing tourists.

Later that evening we ate ice cream,
found a place with a band, drank rum and coke,
Judy danced with me in her blue Hawaiian dress,
(the only time we ever did).

Another evening we listened—
as famous celebrities serenaded us
at a park concert, (beside the zoo
where 150 year old turtles
cocked their heads), and it poured rain
twenty minutes between sets of
James Taylor, then Joni Mitchell.

Enjoying my leave
from the Marines, we mix
with wealthy Americans
at an island Hula dance,
a young native in a grass skirt danced
with flowers in her hair.

Hibiscus flowers in
red or yellow blossoms, are worn
behind the right ear, only if
she is single.
Hula dancers' silky black hair
swayed down to their knees.

A rhythm
they danced with
was as gentle as
waves at Waikiki

Splashing Water

I can paint with words.

I can put a red dot on canvas
or in that space a blue swash.

I can walk down streets of Madrid
or Paris at midnight,
and I can stand on
Waikiki beach
with a surfboard
in my hand.

I can snorkel before sunset
stunned by beautiful fish
utterly amazed at
the Pacific discovery.

I can bicycle across
the Golden Gate Bridge
or up to the peak of
Diamond Head Mountain.

And I can dance with light.

Girls Surfing

Growing up without a father
I tried to change the cycle by
young daughters.

But it was impossible to change
without a grandfather.
Something was always missing.
Fortunately, I had four girls,
two in the first marriage.

After the first divorce
their mother was awarded our girls,
then she remarried. We drifted away.

Due to an incurable illness
my second marriage left me
alone with two lovely girls.

We read out loud, played in snow,
enjoyed movies, sang songs.

Wish now—I could be
with all my daughters
in Oahu, Hawaii
out in the surf.

Honolulu Days

Walking to a nearby playground
with our young daughters
Crystal three, and Cynthia two,
and their mother Judy was relaxing fun.
We always enjoyed going to that park.

At home I studied sociology—
taking a correspondence course offered
through the University of Michigan—graded by
the prof who'd written the textbook. Honolulu
weekdays: I repaired radios on the marine base.

On weekends we'd go out
in my sky blue Chevy Corvair
shopping at an outdoor mall
to see Hula dancers, and Koi—
a Japanese carp that looks like goldfish.

We'd eat thick roast-beef sandwiches, and go
shopping. I loved the collarless shirts on display.
I wish they'd come back into style.

Sometimes we'd go into the library,
which has a beautiful central
courtyard with palm trees,
and look for new books.
I borrowed and read The Glass Bead Game.

We once watched a TV crew
outside the capitol building
film a scene for Hawaii Five-O

in slow motion, and repeat it
and repeat it, and repeat it . . . .

On the block near our apartment
was a petite, indigenous, market offering
fresh fruit, vegetables, bread, milk and fish.

Pearl Harbor was fifteen minutes away.
If the Japanese hadn't first bombed my base
wiping out 95 percent of our Marine Corps planes,
we would have given them a good fight.

Shapley's Heavenly Bodies

This day December twenty-first
momentous and rare recurring in 20 years,

when Saturn and Jupiter align

and from earth's perspective
they appear close together.

So close their illusion is one planet
every four hundred years

since the birth of Jesus.

Shapley's the first astronomer
who figured out

our exact galactic location,
using math.

Am I dreaming this day?
Surfing in warm waves off Waikiki.

The Surfer Dude
>   *for Kipp Johnson*

In the arc of his life
he always was a poet.
Even in June, with his hair
sun-bleached from surfing,
he remembered his worst wipeout,
in those slamming winter-waves at north shore,
the bulk of the wave thundering foam—his
board snapped in two—crushed in a mile of foam.
Dissolving foam helped float her up.

The tides reclaimed him. Was it only a dream?
The sky was deep orange with a yellow-gold sun.
Unnamed seabirds glided across surface water,
evenly buffooning waves, in rhythm, a playful
school of dolphins added notes to the music
that day he found his perfect wave.

Looking for surf, on an evening
when waves strand naked in the curl,
he caught the wave—firmly
on the board's rough surface—
he slipped into the pipeline.
Accelerating, with his knees slightly bent, a
beautiful blue-green saltwater surrounded him,
he jetted out, ending on the wave's shoulder
as an incredible girl, surfed the pipeline. Then
they walked along the beach carrying surfboards.

ESSAY ON WATER
for Reg Saner 1928 -2021

I

Is the ocean's
salty water potentially potable?
Out of respect
for my thesis advisor
I'll try not to imitate his successful,
intellectual style of articulate writing;
comparing and contrasting our lives is
like comparing and contrasting a constant,
and everlastingly
expanding cumulus above
a yellow desert-cactus blossom.
Although, both he and I
were born in the same
sabbath shire of
downstate Illinois,
where rain always fell heavy
after a loud thunder.
We both played tag—
with friends—
near the Illinois Braille
and Sight Saving School.
We both had a kidney removed.

II

He preferred hiking alone
in the desert
because the wind
didn't have much to say

there, unlike the wind talk heard
in Rocky Mountain aspen groves.
And the original desert dwellers—
Anasazi—always built
their incredible habitat
near water.
When Reg put a letter into my file
arguing against continuing
for the doctorate I thought, "that is narrow minded";
I now realize
it was compelled by his fatherly facet
his reason:
"He has two small daughters to provide for."

III

He and I are graduates of Illinois University.
He in Champaign; me in Springfield,
then known as "the Berkeley"
of the Midwest. He accepted a Fulbright
and studied in Italy;
I refused the Illinois Fulbright offer, from Professor
Dennis Camp who was also the curator of
the Vachel Lindsay House, so I
did not go to Paris to write poems.
I always felt guilty about Professor Camp
when I learned of his suicide
thinking, "If I only had accepted the Fulbright,
would he be alive today?"

IV

If I had, I might not be in Colorado.
Reg Saner might not have been my professor.

He wrote "Essay on Air," and "Essay on Earth."
And so I carry on with "Essay on Water."
Oh, but I love the way "Essay on Earth," contains
the words: the sound "say" and the visual "ear."
And people always mispronounce names.
Strangers call him "Sane-r," but
he called himself "S-honer."
Because I knew him I hear his voice
when I read his essays and poems.
So you might ask, "What on earth
does this have to do with water?"

V

That's what I'd like to know.
Back when I was a grad student
Reg came to my poetry reading,
introduced himself to me.
I enjoyed his writing courses.
Six years after I'd graduated
he invited me to go with him to a
reading in Denver.
Afterwards he introduced me
to Mary Oliver.
I'd been teaching at
a Denver university.
Shortly afterwards I
received a call from
an English department
administrator saying
I could now come and register
for doctoral level courses—
I didn't go back thinking,
"I was too old."

VI

In this "Essay on Water,"
and in the desert west now
water's a diminishing desperado.
Buffalo wallows, ponds, creek beds,
more sand than water.
Reservoirs. Shrink into wavy lines of dry air.
Cumulus collapse into blue
disappear, like a candleflame in a mine
out of oxygen.
Drinkable water . . .
decreases and decreases,
as the earth keeps on cracking and drying up.
Oh, yes there's, "Water water everywhere,"
rising in surf around the globe
steadily and steadily on the rise.

Surf Returns
> "I have spread my dreams under your feet; tread
> softly because you tread on my dreams."
> —William Butler Yeats

1

After meeting Janice at a spring dance
she gave me her number;
a week later I invited her out
to my Senior Banquet, and a movie.
She was a cheerleader,
a junior at Franklin High in Illinois;
I was a student at Jacksonville High School
only ten miles away.
Overjoyed she agreed when I asked,
"Do you know someone for my friend Larry
who might join us?"
He drove a new 1968 Road Runner
it was yellow with the best V8 engine
Plymouth ever made.
We gathered that evening
at the Black Hawk restaurant and then
went to the Illinois Theater afterwards
in an impressive Road Runner
to enjoy Dustin Hoffman's second
film performance The Graduate.

2

Life has a unique trajectory for everyone.
At the refreshment counter
selling popcorn, soft drinks, and candy,
was a very cute girl in a gold dress
(all theater staff had dorky uniforms)
she caught my eye for the first time;
and although I didn't know it then,

that young woman would become my wife.
Larry helped me find a job
it seemed nobody would hire
me because of the draft.
I worked with him, and with the daddy
of the girl I'd seen at the theater.
I went to Janice's Homecoming Dance.
We had a date Thanksgiving,
at Christmas, her family invited us
to attend Catholic services with them.
But on Valentine's Day,
ironically while sitting on a bench
at MacMurray College in Jacksonville
she said, "You work in a clothing factory,
ironing men's suits. After graduation
I'm going to college in Springfield;
I cannot see any future with you,
I want to break up."

3

When my draft notice arrived
on my nineteenth birthday
I went to the recruiter's office in Springfield
and joined the marines.
Another friend helped me find a job
at the Kodak film development office
and I began working at night
with a job I enjoyed more—
developing photographs.
Judy, the girl in the gold dress,
yes, the girl in the gold dress and I married.
In October I went to San Diego
for twelve weeks of boot camp.
When training ended I went home
for a month of liberty.

I returned to San Diego
the marines were assigning me
to a naval school for electronics.
When our daughter Crystal
was one month old, Judy
followed me out to San Diego.

4

After I was sent to radio engineering school
during my three-year appointment,
I graduated near the top of my class,
marines brilliantly permitted a commanding officer
in an infantry company to request
a radio repairman be assigned with his men.
That year while stationed at Oceanside, California
Cynthia our second daughter
was born St. Patrick's Day.

5

A couple of times
I asked my commanding officer,
"What is my job in your company,
and why do you want me here?"
His reply was, "Because I can."
I went up in a helicopter
and dropped empty bombshells
tossing them out the tail end
from 2,000 feet every day,
was flown down to those
dug them out of the ground then
put them in the jeep to bring back.
So I went to talk with a lieutenant colonel,
(and why a colo has the kur sound
has always bewildered me because

kernel, which has the exact same sound as
colonel, is a grain or a seed). Now that's ironic.
And the colonel, called the base sergeant-major,
and he sent me over to his office two blocks away,
while they were still talking on the phone.
When they finished talking—
the sergeant major and I chatted for an hour.
He then cut orders for me to go
To work in a radio repair shop
just down the street.

6

He'd offered to cut my orders anywhere I chose,
and I decided to stay in Oceanside.
Six months later
he sent me orders
to work at the marine air base
in Kaneohe Bay, Hawaii.
It was there I began surfing. I also body surfed and
snorkeled in Oahu's blue-green waters.
Once a month the marines made us
run three miles for time,
and hike twenty-five miles
dressed in full battle gear.
Simply walking in Hawaii
made anybody sweat but
hiking double-time with a metal helmet,
a full backpack, wearing long sleeves
and utility trousers, felt like
being drenched in a shower.
From the air base
my electronics company
went on board ship sailing back
to the sandy beaches of Southern California
joining six-thousand other marines

for a two-week assault
war games hitting the beach at Oceanside,
but there was no enemy in sight.
Camping in the mountains,
which gently rolled into bigger blue mountains
was a memorable experience especially
on that 192 square mile base
at night when the stars shown down.

7

On Oahu after six months
Judy decided she had been away from
home and family for nearly three years,
and she went back to Jacksonville in March.
My enlistment didn't end until October.
So I went from our apartment in Honolulu
back to living on base with marines
at Kaneohe Bay where fighter jets
flew overhead daily and surfing was better.
I became ill and was in the island's
army hospital where I recovered,
I was sent to an education office
on the top floor with a civilian
educator who worked there, she told me
how I could apply to college.
So I applied to Lincoln Land College.
Funny thing was I grew up two blocks
from MacMurray and dreamed of
attending college, always thinking
I was too dumb to succeed,
and too poor to afford it.
At my discharge time in August
(the marines let me out six-weeks early)
I began school in Springfield.
Judy was not interested in moving with me.

My first girlfriend left,
thinking I wasn't college material;
my second girlfriend, my wife,
refused to come with me to college,
a hometown girl, she
couldn't escape the pull.

8

Six months before I graduated
from Illinois University with
majors in anthropology and English
I married a second time.
Maureen and I were blessed
with two more beautiful girls
Spirit and February.
Maureen became ill
she went to live at her father's house
in Champaign,
then she was hospitalized,
and moved into a nursing home.
I became a single parent
moved to Boulder working
my way through grad school.

9

Writing came natural
to me and I wrote at night
deep in the midnight hours
starting in Hawaii and continuing
through college and until this moment.
Growing up I could hear hourly bells
from a clock at the top of
MacMurray College library
two blocks away,

and dreamed of being a collegian.
The college opened in 1850
as an elite women's college
with riding stables
a gorgeous collegiate church
a soccer field in the same campus area.
In 1950 they became co-ed.
Four months ago
after 170 years they closed forever.

Things change
a hospital's demolished
and a Catholic church is built in that space;
streets around the town square changed,
theaters and restaurants close,
twelve factories close or move
a state prison is built
in my home town.
In Colorado daughters go to college
marry and live their own lives.
I quit my day job and move to Santa Monica,
thinking of that great weather
of my youth in the marines in California,
but it rained nearly every day.
A friend Betty and I went out to rent a movie
Dustin Hoffman was shopping in the store
looking to rent a movie too.
Many stars live in Santa Monica.
I wrote a dozen or so poems
at the beach, every day watching
surfers or colorful sunsets when possible;
I stayed away from the cold water
and it never occurred to me to surf,
or to write about surfing,
so I returned to Colorado.

10

February, my youngest daughter
bought an Alpha Romero convertible
when she was in high school.
She drove it going to college
and took it to Albuquerque,
where she lived with her husband Kipp
who was a captain in the air force.
She called me and gave that car to me.
And that car was named after a film
because Dustin Hoffman drove
a red Alpha Romero Spider
up and down the Pacific Coast highway
they renamed their Spider The Graduate.
I drove that nearly antique
1984 Graduate seven years,
sold it and used the cash to
travel to China for a job with Jining University.

11

My daughter Crystal
is a graduate of MacMurray
with a degree in business. She has two
daughters, Ashlyn and Reagan. I studied
in an undergrad literature class at MacMurray.
One of the six books I read there
was Dandelion Wine.
A very good magical book.
The professor introduced me to
Gunslinger I & II, poetry books by Ed Dorn
a poet who later would be
one of my grad professors.
My daughter Cynthia
is a graduate of Southern Illinois

with a degree in social work.
My daughter Spirit
is a graduate of Colorado State
with a degree in education
and a grad degree in human resources.
She has one daughter Kayley,
an education senior at Northern Colorado.
Four daughters and three granddaughters
have earned college degrees.
My daughter February
is a graduate of Metropolitan State
with a degree in communication,
as well as a graduate of USC
with a grad degree in social work.

12

Dreams do come true
thoughts become lines
lines become this song
in the grace of moonlight
light shines on my hand
surf returns and I listen
in the quiet stillness
peace reins over war
in the end dreams return
in restful sleep, sound is
song becomes music
a meadowlark sings
out of dark there is light
like sunbeams health rises.

MADRID, CHINA, AND OTHER PLACES

Plaza Mayor Madrid 1974

Small balconies with flowerbeds
cobblestone pavement a parade
men on horseback red plumes bouncing
above their silver helmets
swords and lances, and then
seven and eight year old girls
dressed in white for first communion
followed by a group of chanting monks
and woodcarvings of the king and queen
a group of jesters wearing red and green
troops of boys marching,
and horsemen dressed Elizabethan
set out to discover a new world.

This is Franco's Spain, but today
there is singing in the Plaza Mayor.
After the parade, everyone crowds
into the plaza and the people
lift one voice together in Latin.
Like an electric spark in the air
or a goose chill that's set
down your spine for pure joy
people I'll never know that day
touched me, rubbed shoulders with me,
and their song said, love me, love me.

In center square, the oldest part of town,
many have trundled here: Cervantes,
Hemingway, and Michener. I come here
to eat donuts, and hot chocolate,
in the Red Lion, and to look at the

post office. Years later, two years
after my mother died, I find
a postcard of this place
 by me, but never sent to her.
But I remember her in the joy
of that day of that parade.

A part of the whole that makes up
the modern world, this Mass a throng
singing to the universe
in the land of great cathedrals
and castles protected then
by military police guarding
the streets of the parade.
They could speak to you as you
walked by them. And the Carmelite
sisters, guardians of the Hospital
of Charities, who live with hope.

A metropolis of five million
has grown up around this plaza.
In the plains beyond, olive
and orange groves, and more plains
and mountains, France, Portugal,
Atlantic and Mediterranean border
and shorelines—
the wind blowing up sounds.
Where you can see knights clash
in jousting tournaments
that replicate medieval honor,
crested banners blazing.

And rivers flow here too
surrounding the rock on three sides
where a castle is an
undefeatable fortress looming up.
All of this riding the sound
of the wind or no sound
it is calm in the plaza.
The singing has stopped.
A deep and solemn quiet
overtakes this place
someone is lifting a cup to the blue sky.
Above the soft white petals of the flowerbeds
the silence is broken by the flapping,
brown and white pigeons rise on healing wings,
and the crowd voices, young and old,
all those voices singing.

My College Roommate
       for David Lasley

Like a rare group of birds
building their lofty nests in the same tree
we met at the round table
in the cafeteria, in a room also used
for lectures, dances and concerts.
Previously we had enrolled
in this room to begin our junior classes;
if you enrolled in classes here
you had to commute to a temporary campus.
He was looking for a roommate.
I was looking for a place to live.

Our library was the only building under
construction. This round campus was
built in the center of a cornfield ocean
reaching across the level prairie
as far, in any direction, as you might go;
and hundreds of saplings—with trunks
I could wrap my hand around
were planted encircling our radical
school grounds—
one day they would bloom and mature
spreading their autumn color into clouds.

We rode slowly in an old Dodge, that did not have
brakes, from the low rent two bedroom house
to buy groceries and dog food
with Ed, a seventy-five pound German shepherd
a farm dog blind in one eye with a natural peace
symbol that grew on his furry brown head,

and Arthur, a medium size mutt
with longer silky black hair
who liked to sit up front
with his paws on the dashboard, our watchdog,
as we coasted through stop signs.

David's degree was in music
from Grinnell College, in Iowa,
but he'd decided to return
for a second bachelor's degree
enrolling as a junior;
I was serving in the Marines before
Enrolling at community college,
and then tested out skipping a year.
Entering university we had different paths
to arrive as juniors.
We had four years in common at
Newton Bateman Memorial High
as David liked to call Jacksonville high,
where our senior class
graduated 365 students in 1968,
where we had known each other
but did not have or share one class
together, nor did we take one
course together at Sangamon State University.

While the old Dodge rested in the garage
we hitched rides to class;
David had a friend in Grinnell
with a bike shop and we bought bicycles
we raced to our classes.
Mine was a white Fiorelli ten-speed
that had hand tooled chrome joints.

And we went on bicycle tours.
David invited me to sit in his class being
team taught by Norman Hinton, a lit professor,
and a psychology professor, that focused
on the literature of horror, how the brain
underwent a chemical change as you read it;
that was our single class
and I only went to it one time,
eventually I changed my major.

The summer I went to Spain
when I returned David introduced me to
new music by Chick Corea titled Spain.
I helped David lay a garage foundation at his
parent's to be converted into a shop for his mother.
I once wrote a poem in our living room
while listening to
a soft rain,
play hot jazz, on brilliant green leaves.

Living Inside Confucius Wall

A few Americans have lived here before
in peace and harmony
where moonlight still shines
brilliant orange in October haze.

And along Gu Lou street you may
hear the clomp clomping sound
of old horses pulling tourists
to and from the Confucius Temple.

Here there are intricate
roof patterns and those
ancient eaves built to overlap—

 fill in space, as if sky and eaves
were lovers—touching over and under.

Tigers Of The Chinese Calendar
for Betty Woon

Mirth in the cool summer
more rain than usual
this year and now autumn
comes inch by inch—
this wide earth tilting
at the axis towards winter.
The steady sun blazing
in the short time we have.

A long time ago now it was in
the year of the tiger
a tiger gave birth to two
orange cuddly kittens—
with our silver wire-rimmed
John Lennon glasses
and our blue collar style.
How Hemingwayesque
our meeting in Madrid.

Christ bless us with peace
born on this earth
let there be peace
warm bread
and good wine
and let us laugh together.

Fifteenth Child

Because of fear I have avoided the bear
that stands with paws and claws
upraised. The grizzly turns sniffing
goes through fields of fiery red petals
to a forest with golden aspen leaves
shimmering in the wind.

I packed everything I owned
into my car.
Ten years ago I arrived.
I've watched the blue heron
stand motionless
studying the perfect water.

What are the odds
we are the babies of our families?
She has seven
older brothers and sisters
and in our conversation
she says, "Why am *I* here?"

Every day I ask the same question.

The fifteenth child
is a cutthroat trout swimming
in the clear river, starlight
twinkling at dusk, a snowfall
in the fields. Breaking silence.

Pyromaniac

A holocaust of institution's
destructive power.

Why couldn't the detectives
figure it out?
He always flees the scene
on his Honda,
then returns to carry hoses
from the hook and ladder truck.
A million in damages,
and his picture
on the front page.

The fragrant bouquet of
gasoline splashes—
the igneous magnitude.
Blue flame
blazes from room to room.
He wants to walk out
barefoot,
on coals white hot
to go through fire.

Encounters At The Washing Machine During A Pandemic

People parroting what they've heard on TV:
This Corona Virus is not as bad as the flu.
Flu kills 12,000 people every year.
The democrats are going
to get rid of all the churches;
we have the cleanest air, and
cleanest water in any country.
More people are
dying of heart attacks
now than the virus.
My friend just died
of a heart attack.
He didn't have the virus
he had a blood clot
in his heart.
Veteran's hospitals do not
have any problems
with the Corona Virus.
Lucky he was a veteran.
Power companies
in America
are going to shut off
our electricity
every night
and run everything
on solar and wind power
to try and clean up
the environment.
A lot of countries
will not let Americans
come in anymore.

Integrity

Integrity guides us as individuals
and as a nation. When a leader
is a vile person it can cause
others to become distracted from
their own personal integrity
ever so slightly, but just enough to
cause those others not to do their best.
When a leader lacks honesty
it can cause a relaxation in
the honesty of those who follow.
If a nation lacks integrity that nation
will fall. And oh, how far down
can we go? If it is true—ruthless
men gain only wealth—then what?
Every day we need to do our best,
and uphold integrity!

The Café

Folded cash
mom brought home in a
yellow business card size
envelope pay day
for three decades.

As a waitress
she earned nickel, dime,
and quarter tips
she gave to me for
ice cream and movies.

In our neighborhood
wealthier children
whose two parent families
owned houses and cars
had less pocket change.

Preparing kitchen and coffee,
opening the café each morning,
she arose
before the sun pulled its shoulders
out of bed.

Simpler Days

Nine lines in honor of my mother. She
died before the invention of the cell phone; she
never had a driver's license or owned a vehicle; she
never owned her own home; she
loved to read and take long Sunday walks; she
shared faith and love with family and friends; she
studied Latin and Greek in high school; she
made only A grades all the way through; she
loved one man her whole life. She . . . .

Original Description

First the café where mother worked six-days-a-
week for twenty-six years closed, windows
boarded-up, then the rest of the stores, which
were so much exactly like the city of Bedford Falls

in the film "It's a Wonderful Life," but so very
much exactly worse. Mother made straight A's all
through high school, and that was when Latin and
Greek were normal subjects to study.

My home town has metamorphosed into something
else. It's like a film makers nightmare became real.
I've often wondered why mom never was offered a
scholarship to college, but she graduated in the

1930s and would be 108 if she were only alive
today, but nobody is 108, at least not in my home
town. Science can tell you the human eye is self-
healing, or self-vision correcting with Lasik

surgery, and the human brain is capable of self-
healing the body, perhaps acupuncture stimulates
that, but what is incredible is how many cells in our
body die every three seconds and are replaced with

new cells. Most of our oldest cells aren't that old.
No matter your age, most cells in your body are
fifteen to forty-years old. Original description, you
may be younger than you think you are.

The Umber Haze of Summer

So, like the blue note in a jazz riff, on your first
Gig as a writer, you covered the story of the most
popular writer in the nation of pigment-hating skin
tones.

All the Washington dignitaries were there in their
finest, and you in jeans and a sweater, on the front
row, with a press pass, while NBC, CBS, and ABC
wore 800-dollar suits.

Like a coyote singing to the stars a worthy
complaint, the author walked onstage wearing a
pewter suit, and a smile. The author spoke with
slow confidence having honed

his writing skills for twenty years in the Coast
Guard. He was $200,000 in debt on the Frisco Bay
when he began researching for his roots.
Alex Haley a soft spoken, and

mild mannered man, looked me in the eye saying,
"I believe I'm a conduit of God." Always an
inspiration. Closing, he invited everybody in the
press backstage for a champagne reception.

Epiphany

A delicate speck of lime,
you fly away.
I didn't know that you could,
someday I will.

Erecting A New Memorial

Is covid-19 the earth's way
of cleansing itself?
It has killed more Americans
than the Vietnam War.
It has swept away
the umber haze of summer.

Illinois & Times

Immaculate places
I went as a child
were widescreen
located at the northeast
corner of our town
square, the Illinois,
the Times a block
away, on east main street.
For one quarter, or a dime,
you could see movies such as,
westerns, horror, love stories,
gangsters, comedies, war films,
and funny they always ran a
cartoon before every show.
Inside, the aroma of hot buttered
popcorn, alongside candy or
soda pop in a paper cup
that could drop down
and fill up to the brim with
Orange, Coke or Dr. Pepper.
There were in those theaters
back in grade school, for
example in the dark,
a moist glory in
kissing a lovely girl.

Janet Hard

Her thick British accent was like music on the phone. She sent me an application to the Colorado writing program and gave me her home number. My daughters, six and three, put all we had into

my Ford Galaxy and drove from central Illinois toward the continental divide. I had very little money and arranged free lodging in Kansas with a family someone knew at a church.

By the time we pulled into Boulder I had just enough cash in my pocket to buy a package of hot dogs on sale at Safeway. It was 6:30 p.m. on the 6th of August 1981 when I went to Regent Hall,

which was closed, and the bright sunny campus seemed deserted. As we walked to the University Memorial Center I recall thinking there wasn't a band playing welcoming the poet from Illinois.

I phoned Janet. She invited us out to her home, let us sleep in her camper, and cooked fresh eggs from her chickens every morning for two weeks until I found a job. We had a majestic view of the

snowcapped peaks along the front range; and Janet had a black horse she called Lucy my daughters enjoyed riding bareback. While in grad school working on my writing, Janet told me,

"When you have your first book published I will
dance on my desk for you." She had a large
window in her office. It opened outward and she
loved to feed squirrels. One squirrel loved her so

much it jumped on her head. Going to grad school
taught me about the golden thread in my writing.
The day I defended my thesis she offered me a glass
of brandy in her office, then on graduation day

she sat with my daughters in the audience while I
enjoyed the pomp and circumstance and the band
played on. Without her help and encouragement,
I may not have made it through the program.

Janet was a bright light twinkling on my path.
We often ate our sack lunches together on campus.
Janet and Don her husband had four children.
They invited us to celebrate Boxing Day.

Her son must have been impressed because Janet
said he had named his son after me. Once Janet and
I walked across campus removing swastikas from
sidewalks. Six years after graduation, I returned to

her office to share news of my first book; with tears
welling up in her eyes, she said, "Don fell to his
death hiking alone in the Rockies. Saying goodbye
at the funeral, she gave him one last kiss.

Joy

What joy if I were your child?
What joy if I were always your child?

Running galloping charging wild stallions
running blue over this level free prairie.

Four large inland seagulls walking around.

What joy if I wrote poems?
What joy if I always wrote poems for you?

Leo

Standing tall with pride and powerful legs,
a thoroughbred, white with red brindle spots.

An english bulldog a
                              seventy-five pounder.

A pure lightning quick love bundle running to
every child and person wiggling with joy just

to rub up against you
                              happy always to see you

curling his baby Yoda like ears in his exuberance.
Massaging his ribs I felt his last heartbeat.

Emerald Rainbow

different
and fresh

as the mourning dove sings

above the clear waterfall.
Oh yes

thoughts splinter
into rivers

trying to describe
what cannot be seen.

For your eyes there's
no second expression,

jazz sax whole notes a rhythm
singing phrases that reach home.

This sizzling green arc of unique color
at first light so morning just.

Pie

Apple cherry blackberry, rhubarb
as in where the world began
peach pumpkin pecan, coconut,
banana-cream with golden-brown meringue
in your grandma's early morning kitchen
let your eyes shut
inhale the miraculous aromas
taste the sweetest strawberry . . .
whipped, beat, peeled, stirred,
baking powder, flour flurries, for example
melt in your mouth crust, rolling pin thin;
banana-cream with real banana slices
and things such as cinnamon, allspice, nutmeg
all revolve around the center, her creation
of pie, wonderous pie, halleluiah pie!

Spoon River

It was a misty morning, May was in full bloom. I
did not know I'd one day eat beignet in New
Orleans. I did not know I would sail underneath the
Golden Gate Bridge in San Francisco twice in

my life. Nor did I know I would be stationed at
Kaneohe Bay Marine Air Base for a year in the time
of Vietnam. How could I? At the time I was only
eleven. The river babbled a melodious and

soothing sound as it meandered around and over
curved stones, washed along the current uncount-
able years. It was one of two twenty-five mile hikes
I would complete as a scout, the other was

at Cahokia, both in Illinois. Which hike came first?
I do not recall. And what I remember of my home
place, in a small community, is the land was flat.
You could see the horizon in any direction.

The sky was big. Thunder could rattle the
windows. The river was a unique landscape with
leafy trees crowding the trail. We went in mist and
out of fog and the sun did not show it's brilliant

face, all day. We walked along the many curved
turns and twists in the shallow river. And among
the close knit group of youth who walked with me
that day, three would lose their lives in Vietnam.

The 1966 24-Hour Le Mans Trophy

Cruising in a zone,
no cars in front,
 no cars behind—
a slot-car track
opened in my hometown;
I bought a car kit
a replica 1966 Ford GT40,
painted the body pink
and put Pink Panther
decals on the car—
cruising on that circular track an
older fellow offered me twice its value,
I gave him my Pink Panther.
Our hometown YMCA held a
slot-car drag racing contest;
one week after I sold it
the Pink Panther took
their 1st place trophy.
Earlier in 1966 Ken Miles,
along with Carroll Shelby,
helped Ford build the GT40
and Ken drove it in the rain at
Le Mans breaking the course record
with a lap time of 3 minutes
30.6 seconds, going 218 mph at 7,000 rpm.
Nearing the finish, Ken
held a four minute lead ahead
of two other Ford GT40s following
in second and third place behind him
when upper level company execs
asked if he could slow

down for a photo op, then
all three Ford GTs might cross
the finish line side by side.
So Ken did slow down. French judges
agreed before the finish to grant
Ford a three-way tie; closely observing
the photo finish they reneged,
granting the trophy to a slower GT40
who had won Le Mans in their photo.
My disappointment rankled. Consolation none.
When the slot-car I'd carefully put together
won 1st place in our YMCA's race
knowing he'd built the first three GT40s,
and driven his perfectly, leading the way
in the 1966 24-hour Le Mans,
I can only imagine Ken Miles' vexation.

The Willow

Wrinkled skin
over one-hundred years old
her massive trunk twisted rising
as if sculpted with love.

Roots reach far into
damp soil while
branches muscle up
to places unknown.

She provides for her children,
like a mother, for the northern flicker,
the blue bird, the chickadee,
the robin, the crow.

Wispy thin branches
flow down
touching grass like
strands of blond hair,

they sway
dancing in a gentle breeze,
on the unseen breath
of a warm chinook.

WALKING IN SNOW BEFORE DAWN

Ducklings

The soft patter of rain, on the leaves, woke me this
morning. Sunlight filled the clear sky. I walked, feeling the
cool fresh air, a mountain trail rising through aspen and
       down through lodgepole

pines, to a lake with yellow water lilies blooming. Sitting
on a large flat boulder at the lake, two young brown
ducklings came up onto the rock and sat down beside me.
       Surprising, these wild

creatures demanded part of my lunch. They ate raisins,
sunflower seeds and the pumpkin seeds I shared, and they
sat beside me nibbling at my shirt buttons. Although they
       had feathers and were

siblings, they were alone on the lake. Looked, like about
nearly grown, not yet mature. They behaved as if they had
known me all of their lives, and like that patter of rain, the
       sound I have heard,

which remains the same softly echoing through time.
These two courageous, clear eyed sisters that joined me for
lunch, walking around me, made the day unique as they
       nibbled my fleshy fingers.

Driving A Tractor At Seven
>   Remember me one of your lovers of dreams.
>   —Carl Sandburg

Waking at four a.m. to walk 250 cows from the pasture to
the barn for their morning milking was my daily chore
on a dairy farm in Cherry Valley. I was spending the

summer with my sister and her husband. He would take
me out in the field on the tractor for the rest of the day.
He taught me how to drive the tractor as I rode along.

He had me steering long before he taught me how to
operate it. I knew how to start the ignition, how to shift
gears, how to use the throttle, how to use the brakes.

One afternoon he stopped cultivating the corn, and then
asked me if I would run back to the barn, drive a tractor
parked there back to him. So I ran across the field and

down the dirt and gravelly road that wound its way back
into the barn. I climbed on the tractor and drove it back to
him. He climbed on and asked me to return the tractor

he was using back to the barn. I did but I wanted to see
how fast it could go, so I shifted it into high gear, racing
it back. On a 45 degree turn the tractor balanced up on

two wheels around the corner, then fell back down on all
four wheels, as I drove it safely back into the barn. In the
evening, and for the remainder of the summer, my driving

privileges were suspended. Some older farm boys taught
me to play baseball in their backyard. Throwing wild
fastballs, the pitcher hit me in the forehead. I felt dazed,

and had a knot over my eye the size of a goose egg. It's the only injury I suffered that summer. And at seven I never dreamed about playing baseball or driving a tractor.

If the tractor tipped over it might have killed me. I enjoyed playing pony league ball, played center field in the Marine Corps, a turning point. Health held me hitless. My kidney

failed and was removed by doctors. As I recovered
I began waking at night, writing poems. Writing
poems became my real FIELD OF DREAMS dream.

Columbine
> *After Sandburg's "Grass"*

Pile the bodies high at Columbine and Parkland.
Shovel them under and let me work—
     I am public education; I teach all.

And pile them high at Sandy Hook
And pile them high at Red Lake and Virginia Tech.
Shovel them under and let me work.
One year, twenty years, parents and students ask their
legislators:
     Why are guns legal?
     Why are automatic guns available?

     I am education.
     Let me work.

The face of the river by night holds a scatter of stars . . . .
—Carl Sandburg

And What Truth Makes Something Out Of Nothing?

As a boy I sat one evening
in the public library
a vision of a midnight sky
blazing a galaxy of stars in my eyes
and a notion of equality in death
death truly is democratic
it accepts everybody old and young alike
poor and rich and on that day—
red blood is never flowing inside
from white bones—everyone has bones
and shall become equally silent . . .
& a spirit giving life moves on in
the face of the river by night.

Baseball

1964 my first tryout for pony league, we stood in the outfield catching fly balls, then hit a few in batting practice. Fortunately, *Hertzburg New Method Book Bindery* coach
      wanted me to play

right field. I made the cut. Our uniforms were white with blue caps and blue socks. Our team won every game that summer. I was anticipating entering high school in the fall.
      When we played

Coca-Cola for the city championship, our season had ended undefeated. As a reward our team went to St. Louis to watch the *Cards* play the *San Francisco Giants*. It was my
      first major league

baseball game. I was one of those kids that never had a catch with his father. I never knew him. My older brother Gary showed me how to throw a knuckle and a curve ball.

Gary went to the *Cards* game with me as a team chaperone. The funny thing was no one from my family ever came to the park to watch me. I rode my bicycle there and back
      alone, each game.

Micro Screenplay

scene
east of the sun and west of the moon

sociology professor and catholic priest
you are not writing sociology

student
if it's not sociology what is it

soc prof
its literature

grad level literature professor visiting from england
you will never write a screenplay

student
ok if you say so

angel
blessed are those who are invited to the
wedding supper of the lamb

2020 Census

I have the untenable assignment
trying to change the paradigm
of ignoramuses who are rude and abusive
that think the Census is a waste: of their
time, and of government money.
Those who hang up the phone
and will not talk with you;
or those who say, "I'm on vacation
and don't want to think about it."
Personally I long for the days
when I was young and carefree
and had time every day
to catch a wave and surf it
on the east side of Kaneohe Bay, Hawaii,
where avoiding sharks and jellyfish was
decidedly more exciting than dealing with
really dumb stupid white racist
Americans who love the flag
more than they will ever love people.

Cello & Guitar

I'm the only daughter in my family;
in our old school where they had potlucks,
the floors were blond hardwood,

I like to take my cello there
when no one else
is around, and bliss
                        out playing

music. This guy came in and
strummed his guitar playing chords
with me as I practiced.

It was like I understood I was not alone,
I was not meant to play solo all the time.
Playing together was like flying.

Now we play in my two favorite cities
in January we perform in New Orleans, and
then in June we perform in San Francisco.

And this is a dream, playing the cello
and performing with a guitar player.
When the light of dawn comes I awake.

Bunny

Obsidian hair covers her body except for tan eyeliner
around each shiny brown eye, and there is another thin tan
line beneath her chin from the side, which looks like a
        gorgeous necklace. She lives free

in my granddaughter's room. When I go into her room I
always give Bunny a small dish of whole oats and sit
beside her on the floor reading. She gobbles the oats
        making sounds with her teeth.

She cannot wait for me to set the dish down. She always
comes to me and always eats the oats contentedly until they
are gone. Then she will come to where I am reclining
        against a huge tiger and rest

her head on my arm. Or she will nuzzle my hand to pet
her. Kayley named her Bunny. She has tan fur in her
pliable ears, snug curves. A glorious part of the symphony
        in this universe.

At First Light
>   *for John and Peggy Knoepfle*

Clear and visible
in the dark sky,

only Venus reflects the sun
under constellations
that cannot be seen.

Sprinting in the park
on a grassy oval.
The old willow's skirt is wet

where fairies touched down.
A rabbit nibbles in a meadow of dew.

Mourning doves they don't
dance in a ring like mushrooms.

Apache

Megan the wrangler from Illinois
brought the red and white stallion
paint she called Apache
out for me to saddle up.

But today we didn't see beaver—
only sharply chewed pine stumps.
And she galloped her frisky palomino
Sea Four along the beaver dam.

Balanced Rock

You go down Devil's Gulch
a piece, to reach the trail head
where a path leads up
between two fences. Property
lines drawn in barbed wire.
A shallow creek crosses
the dirt trail. I waded through,
and saw my first dead elk.
No more than five yards
beyond my right hand—
thick reddish brown fur
covered the carcass
except where white bones
of the rib cage were exposed,
and most of the neck was gone.
I figure eighteen inches of snow
made the coyotes ravenous.
They ate their fill and left the rest
for birds or maybe that elk
died of old age.
Up a few bends the trail
has boulders all around and
stairs made of pink salt and pepper
granite. Sand and gravel upwards climbing
nine-hundred feet for over two trail miles.
With spectacular turns
and magnificent views;
at Gem Lake—where most
hikers pause to rest then
turn back. Just across
the sandy shore of Gem Lake

is another narrow trail head
that curves around and down
north, then west to Balanced Rock.
Relatively level this trail
has hundreds of fallen pines.
Some snapped like twigs
in howling winter winds,
in varying stages of decay.
While aspen and pine seedlings
flourish here I follow
this trail with no sign of footprints
until the trail disappeared
into forest floor.
I tread lightly and really—
I don't know the way to where I am going.
When I look up though
I thought, "This must be the place."
A huge oval shaped boulder faced me,
on a pinnacle, weighing several tons.
I wondered "how," and "why"
it stands here uniquely, and will be—
years after I'm not here.

On Deer Mountain

Heavy snow forecasted.
Kirk says, "I've never seen
snow falling here—
it's always blowing sideways."

A park ranger says,
"Deer Mountain has
36 inches fresh snow—
makes it hard to see the trail.

With clouds low
and sideways snow where I go up
from the trail head,
a golden eagle circles above me.

Sunshine comes out
on this jagged mountain peak
as the winter storm rages
along the continental divide.

Boulders are warm and dry
at the mountain crest.
I stop and eat a turkey sandwich and a cookie.
A couple from Ohio come and take my photo.

Pile Burning

Lodgepole pines growing thick
their tops sway peacefully.
My grounds crew for pile burning
wore hard hats fireproof clothing
and zipped gators over our boots.
Carrying: shovels and extra gloves,
a fuel can and drip burner
and boxes of kitchen matches.
We drove the two-ton dump truck
slowly winding our way up Emerald
Mountain working for the YMCA.
Then we hiked through snow
with our lunch sacks and water
to piles of pines cut and stacked last summer.
We dug logs out brushing off the snow;
all day we put the wet logs on roaring bonfires,
flames and smoke licking our eyes and skin.
A giant raven flew down at lunch
and walked around. And swerved skillfully
away wheeling through the swaying pines.
We stoked those flaming fires obediently, burning
twenty-five piles in fourteen blazes. Near the fires
large circles of snow retreated into steam.
Two investigative chickadees arrived
as we shoveled snow onto live coals
until flames ceased and smoke
disappeared in the western wind.

Reporting My Pint To The IRS

Without any real figures
near another year's end
Saturday at Conner O'Neill's Pub,
and the Irish dancers
fling their legs high.

Aggressive optimism
bold explosive heels and toes
leaping across the stage while—
the red-haired boy
is smothered with kisses.

Quick rhythmic taps
for ballerina toes, and their red traditional
dresses whirling as they kick and turn,
tapping and leaping around the floor
for another frothy pint of ale.

A leprechaun in a kelly green shirt with a
white beard sips his pint, then quietly leaves.
And lovely Irish dancers spring high leg kicks
far above their glistening eyes while—
the red-haired boy is smothered with kisses.

Twin Sisters Mountain Peak

11,435 feet at the top.
Today I am hiking
Twin Sisters in the Rockies.
Bear claw marks in ponderosa bark,
wind talking loudly over 60 mph,
and I'm in oxygen debt.
I find a spot in the curve
of the craggy peak
out of the freezing wind.
Takes me 40 minutes
to eat lunch and a small bag of gorp.
A tall thin couple from the Czech Republic
play on the rocks across from me;
they had passed me at the tree line,
and were eating when I
climbed to the top.
Earlier I'd rubbed aspen bark—
a whitish powder—on my face
as a sun block, the way Native Americans have
back before we settled on their
sacred hunting grounds.
On the ascent there were: four grey squirrels,
three friendly chickadees.
The trail was snow-packed and treacherous
ice-pack from trail head to peak
where the snow was deepest.
Large ravens circled overhead
gliding on wind currents
rasping their awful song.

Walking In Snow Before Dawn

A doe browsing in juniper
with a mouthful of leaves
lifts her ears, but doesn't
startle the sky which is
baby blue and deep

snow packs underfoot squeaks
like someone sleeping
who grinds the teeth.

A narrow trail down canyon
is untouched by
the first light of morning.

"Publishing books people love reading."

Burning Daylight (imprint)

Ikaria, a Love Odyssey on a Greek Island, Anita Sullivan.
Black 14, Ryan Thorburn.
I Look Around for my Life, John Knoepfle.
Cowboy Up, Ryan Thorburn.
It Started & Ended, Bud Grounds.
Lost Cowboys, Ryan Thorburn.
The Bridge of Isfahan, Nilla Cram Cook.
Ever After, Anita Sullivan.
The Border War, Ryan Thorburn.
Men of the Inland Rivers, John Knoepfle.
Swinging Away a Celebration, Victor Pearn.
Adventures of a Footloose Hippie, George M. Eberhart.

Indian Paintbrush Poets (imprint)

Walking in Snow, John Knoepfle.
Then She Kissed El Paco's Lips or April in Dekalb,
    Ricardo Mario Amezquita.
Shadows and Starlight, John Knoepfle.
The Aloe of Evening, John Knoepfle.
Mad Blood, Jim Keller and Murray Moulding, Editors.
Apricot Harvest, Victor Pearn.
Lullaby of Love, Rebecca Winning.
Essay on Water, Victor Pearn

www.ingramcontent.com/pod-product-compliance
Lightning Source LLC
Chambersburg PA
CBHW052215240426
43670CB00037B/632